HOW MONSTERS WISH TO FEEL

How Monsters Wish to Feel is a therapeutic story about a journey to develop emotional resilience. Through the analogy of monsters, it depicts a tale of how a child's needs can sometimes become distorted, so that the needs we see expressed through outward behaviour (the monster) mask the true, hidden emotional needs that go unmet. The story also alludes to the importance of focusing on the strengths and protective factors in a child's life, rather than the problems and risks, in order to promote emotional resilience. This beautifully illustrated storybook will appeal to all children, and can be used by practitioners, educators and parents as a tool to discuss emotional resilience with children.

Juliette Ttofa is a Specialist Senior Educational Psychologist with 15 years' experience working with children and young people. She specialises in supporting resilience and well-being in vulnerable children.

Julia Gallego is a picture book illustrator and designer, and a graduate of the Manchester School of Art.

For Jason & Evie
X

With acknowledgements to Hans Christian Andersen for the line
"eyes as wide as saucers" from the *"Tinder Box"*
story and the phrase "twinkling foam" from the poem
"Winkin', Blinkin' and Nod" by Eugene Field
– both of which my dearest Dad read to me so often
when I was a wide-eyed child.

I would also like to acknowledge the ending lines of the story: "to feel
themselves beloved on the earth" which is inspired by the poem "Late
Fragment" by Raymond Carver.

How Monsters Wish to Feel

A Story About Emotional Resilience

Juliette Ttofa

Routledge
Taylor & Francis Group

LONDON AND NEW YORK

Illustrated by Julia Gallego

First published 2018 by Routledge
2 Park Square, Milton Park, Abingdon, Oxon OX14 4RN

52 Vanderbilt Avenue, New York, NY 10017

Routledge is an imprint of the Taylor & Francis Group, an informa business

© 2018 Juliette Ttofa

Illustrations © 2018 Julia Gallego

British Library Cataloguing-in-Publication Data
A catalogue record for this book is available from the British Library

Library of Congress Cataloging-in-Publication Data
A catalog record for this title has been requested

ISBN 13: 978-1-909301-84-9 (pbk)

Typeset in Calibri
by Apex CoVantage, LLC

In the heart of a forgotten forest, the River Monsters drink
at streams they say we can't drink from.
And carry strange cups close to their chests.

1

One restless Monster, muddled and slapdash,

darts hare-brained to the river.

He trips on tree roots and out

sploshes the water from his bashed-up cup.

Another Monster is in a blind panic.

Afraid that her chipped cup may never stay full,

she burrows into the bank like a frightened mole,

and clings anxiously to the water's edge.

The third Monster, green-eyed with jealousy,
doubts his thirst will ever be satisfied.
Slyly as a fox, he guzzles greedily from others' cups,
and his own fragile container is left empty.

4

One lonely Monster, stray as a cat,

silently seals-up her sorry cup so nothing will seep out.

But she lets nothing in and wanders

bravely about the endless forest

yearning for a refreshing

drink.

5

Then the angry Monster bulldozes through,
gnashing his teeth like a dog.
His leaky cup can never be filled and
he roams madly around the river bank,
brandishing his cup like a sword.

Yet another worried Monster, tormented with thirst,

is compelled to check his cup for flaws.

He squirrels to and fro like a yo-yo,

too caught up with problems to take a drink.

Lastly, the saddest Monster of all is as hungry as a she-wolf.

Her lips are chapped and her cup is cracked.

She howls hopelessly beside the murkiest part of the river

and sips, cup-less, from its dangerous depths...

I ran with the River Monsters one night. Watched their circus play:

Wild as the wind they spun. Eyes as wide as saucers. Tongues as dry as dust.

That was the night of the great Flood.

Rain Fell Hard.

Roads became Rivers.

And the River burst its banks...

The torrent swept away the Monsters.

Bits of debris crashed around them and in the chaos they clung onto their cups for dear life.

The Monsters roller-coastered along raging rapids; they death-slid down steep flumes.

They were mangled through dark, rocky ravines, and finally tumbled out onto a shore far, far away.

The bedraggled monsters, tangled up in tree roots, nestled together by some cliffs for warmth. In desperation, they trailed a message in the wet silt; the saddest creature put a note inside a bottle and cast it far out to sea. Silent tears fell, like grains of sand through time. Then came a stillness. The storm had passed and there was peace. Tame and weary, the soft sounds of the sea lulled the monsters into a
deep, deep, sleep...

...Days and days passed.

Plentiful tides poured in and sifted out.

The monsters' cups rolled and gambolled

about on the briny shore-line, like flotsam and jetsam,

until all sharp edges were rounded-off,

and their surface became as soft and smooth as sea-glass.

13

A small Silkworm, no bigger than a thumb,
inched its way towards the cups.

Little by little, it spun a shimmering thread of
silk and repaired each cup, one by one,

leaving gleaming seams of gold,
where there had once been only brokenness.

Then one night, when the full-faced moon hung high, the stars burst into the sky so brightly that they seemed to ring like tiny crystal-bells. And the monsters awoke.

They glimpsed their gilded cups, now glinting brilliantly in the moonlight like lost treasure, and gazed towards the starlit-sea with wonder. It made their hearts sing, and, making a wish upon a star, they drank in the beauty as boundless as a healing well.

15

On the horizon, a friendly lighthouse
winked its sparkly eye: illuminating the darkness
with a sudden wand of white.

The monsters splashed their faces in the twinkling foam,
and, as they stared down,

the stars' reflections slipped away to reveal the image
of seven pairs of blinking eyes:

And   Seven   Smiling   Children.

Then it was a new day. And it dawned on me:

The monsters had been in the forest for so long,

they had forgotten they weren't monsters after all;

Just very thirsty children, so bothered by their thirst,

that they couldn't fill their cups.

And who from behind their monster masks,

longed to call themselves beloved.

To feel themselves beloved on this earth.

This is how *all* monsters wish to feel.